Balloon Voyage

THE GREAT ADVENTURES SERIES
Balloon Voyage

Rupert Saunders

Rourke Enterprises, Inc.
Vero Beach, Florida 32964

**Artists impression of the Virgin
Atlantic Flyer**

LIBRARY OF CONGRESS
Library of Congress Cataloging-in-Publication Data

Saunders, Rupert, 1951-
  Balloon voyage/By Rupert Saunders.

  p. cm. — (Great adventure series)
  Includes index.
  Summary: Describes how, in 1986, Richard Branson
and Per Lindstrand became the first persons ever to
cross the Atlantic Ocean by hot air balloon.
  ISBN 0-86592-870-3
  1. Balloon ascensions — Juvenile literature.
2. Transatlantic flights — Juvenile literature.
3. Branson, Richard — Juvenile literature. 4. Lindstrand
Per — Juvenile literature. [1. Balloon ascensions.
2. Transatlantic flights. 3. Branson, Richard.
4. Lindstrand, Per.]I. Title. II. Series:
TL621.V57S28 1988   88-12211
629.13'09111 - dc19   CIP
                  AC

CONTENTS

The Plan

In August 1986 a young British millionaire, Richard Branson, led a team of adventurers to set a new world record for crossing the Atlantic Ocean from America to England in a boat. For many hundreds of years, explorers have raced to be the first or the fastest to cross it.

Richard Branson's powerboat, the *Virgin Atlantic Challenger II*, set a time of three days, eight hours, and 31 minutes for the Atlantic crossing. It traveled from New York harbor to Bishops Rock Light, off the coast of Ireland.

Apart from being a man who loves adventure, Richard Branson is also very successful in business. In Britain he owns a large record company, several nightclubs, and an airline, Virgin Atlantic. Having set a record for crossing the great ocean by sea, Branson began to look for a new challenge.

That challenge was brought to him by a fellow adventurer and ace pilot, Per Lindstrand. Lindstrand was born in Sweden but moved to England, where he owns a company that makes hot air **balloons**. As one of the best hot air balloon pilots and designers in the world, Per Lindstrand was working on a plan to fly one of his own balloons across the Atlantic.

Richard Branson and Per Lindstrand

The Virgin Atlantic Flyer route:
Black dots show the position
Red marks show wind speed
and direction

ONDON - MIA
Fly
Virgin
atlantic
Virgin
LONDON · NEW YORK
MIAMI · EUROPE

In theory, such a journey was impossible. The design of existing hot air balloons could not carry sufficient gasoline to fly for 3,000 miles, the distance across from America to Europe. Winds across the sea are dangerous and unpredictable. But Lindstrand thought he had a plan that would work.

As early as 1873, men have been laying plans to cross the Atlantic Ocean by balloon. Five brave men have died in attempts to make that crossing.

The first modern attempt was in 1958, when Colin Mudie and his family tried from east to west, setting off from Tenerife, one of the Canary Islands off the west coast of Africa. They were in a balloon-boat combination. The boat was used after 1,200 miles of flying, when the balloon crashed, and the family sailed safely on to Barbados.

Others have not been so lucky. Weather conditions in the middle of the Atlantic are extremely dangerous. Any successful crossing relies on careful planning, great technical support, and much luck.

For several months, the two adventurers talked about and planned the flight. Branson was fascinated by hot air balloon flight and the prospect of the Atlantic crossing. Lindstrand understood the dangers and the technical skill that would be needed.

If they succeeded, they would be the first men ever to cross the Atlantic Ocean by hot air balloon. They would have to fly a distance of over 3,000 miles. They would break the existing world record of 907 miles for distance flown in a hot air balloon.

They planned that the flight would take about four days. The existing record for length of flight in a hot air balloon was 27 hours, 23 minutes. If their flight was successful, they would break that record, too.

If they failed, they would probably die.

Richard Branson

The Balloon

The hot air balloon that the two men decided to build was going to be called the *Virgin Atlantic Flyer*. It was to be the biggest balloon ever built in the world, about three-quarters of the size of a football stadium.

All balloons are made up of two main parts; the **envelope** of the balloon, which is used to contain the hot air, and the **basket**, in which the passengers fly. In this case, the basket of the balloon was replaced with a **capsule**, just like a space capsule, so that the crew could survive the long, hard flight.

All balloons fly because the envelope and basket of the balloon float in the air which surrounds them. Just as a ship floats on the sea, so a balloon drifts on a current of air.

Hot air is lighter than cold air; **hydrogen** and **helium** are two gases that are lighter than cold air. If you fill a large-enough balloon envelope with sufficient hot air, hydrogen, or helium, eventually it will float well enough on the cold air around it to lift basket and occupants into the sky.

In order to heat the air in the balloon envelope, **burners** that use **propane** gas are fitted below the open neck of the balloon. When you want the balloon to go up, you turn up the flame from the hot air

Inside the capsule

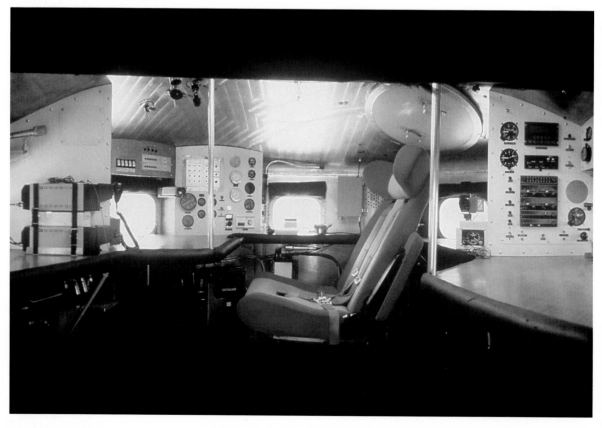

burners. When you want the balloon to go down, you switch the burners off.

All hot air balloons have to carry tanks of propane in order to power the burners. The problem with crossing the Atlantic was that even the biggest balloon in the world could not carry enough propane to keep it in the air the whole way across. Per Lindstrand had an answer.

He planned to use the most powerful heat source in the universe, the sun, to help warm the air in the balloon during the hours of daylight. By designing the balloon to take full advantage of the sun's heat, less propane would have to be carried.

Even with the help of **solar power**, the balloon envelope was going to have to lift a huge amount of its own fuel, plus such vital items as a

Beginning the inflation process

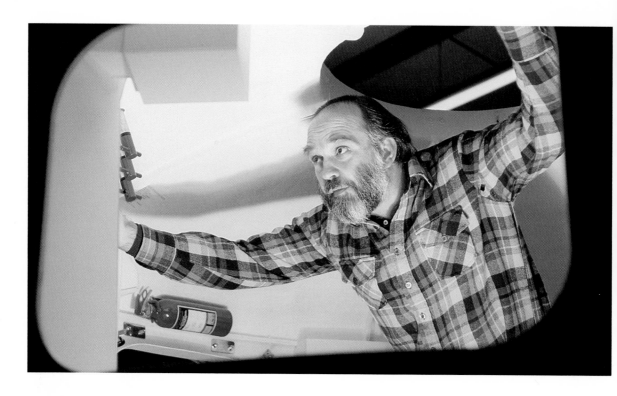

generator to power radio and navigation equipment, the capsule itself, and the weight of the crew.

When fully inflated, the envelope of the *Virgin Atlantic Flyer* had a volume of 2.137 million cubic feet. The envelope alone had a height, from the neck to the top of the dome, of 172 feet, 8 inches and, at its widest point, was 166 feet, 3 inches across.

Just as important to the success of the flight was the design of the capsule in which the crew would travel. The plan was to fly above all the clouds and winds that make most crossings of the Atlantic so rough. But that meant flying above a height of 20,000 feet and giving the pilots a sealed space capsule with its own oxygen and air supply. During the flight, the temperature outside the capsule would be 40 degrees below zero.

Inside the capsule two reclining seats were fitted parallel to each other and facing in opposite directions. One flight station was fitted out as a pilot's position. The other was fitted with navigation and radio equipment. Although either pilot could fly the balloon, during the crossing Per Lindstrand would concentrate on keeping the balloon in the air, while Richard Branson would keep track of position.

At take-off, with gas tanks full and all the systems on board, the *Virgin Atlantic Flyer* weighed over ten tons. The balloon envelope had enough lift to carry a railroad engine into the air and was big enough to cover most of a football field.

The main burners are alight

12

Getting Ready

By September 1986, most of the early work had been finished. It was time to start putting the theory of the flight to the test. Until some actual flying had been completed, the final details of the design would have to wait.

By now Richard Branson was taking an active interest in the balloon. He would have to learn to fly; he would have to learn to survive in the water if they crashed; and he would have to learn **free-fall** parachuting. It was decided to move the whole team to Spain to get some serious testing under way.

New Year's Eve 1986 was celebrated in a small village high on the Spanish central plain. The weather had been foggy and flying the test balloon had not always been possible. But the team members were all very happy with their progress, and Richard Branson's flight training was going well. He was soon mastering the controls necessary to keep balloon and basket in the air.

While Richard learned, the designers were learning too. A capsule and balloon one quarter the size of the final design had been built and were being flown to high **altitude**. The hot air burners performed better than had been expected, but other problems with the capsule design and the material of the balloon itself were discovered. It was time to go back to the drawing board.

By late spring it really seemed as if the dream was going to become real. Project director Tom Barrow, the man in charge of most of the planning of the project, met up with ace weatherman Bob Rice in America to choose a launch site. Meanwhile, Per Lindstrand and Richard Branson began serious training in survival and parachuting techniques.

Laying out the balloon prior to take-off

Test flights over the central plains of Spain

Parachute training will remain a nightmare for Richard Branson. The man who had built a $450 million business empire from nothing in just over 20 years came within inches of death. Freefalling for the first time, he lost control of his flight and began to tumble helplessly towards earth. Only fast reactions by an instructor saved him. In all he completed five parachute jumps, and he hated every one of them.

On the ground things were going better. Tom Barrow and Bob Rice reckoned that they had found the ideal launch site. With the plan to cross from mainland America to Europe, the coast of Maine was the obvious place to look. The actual launch site had to be inland about 100 miles in order to avoid the effects of sea wind.

At **Sugar Loaf** ski resort in Maine the conditions seemed ideal. There were enough comfortable accommodations for the launch crew. The surrounding mountains offered shelter from the wind, and the local authorities were happy to help.

Suddenly, time was running short. In early June the launch equipment, workshop equipment, and mobile communications unit were shipped to Boston by sea. On June 16, the *Virgin Atlantic Flyer* itself and key members of the team took off from London to make the Atlantic journey from east to west.

Two days later, Richard Branson himself flew to Maine to begin launch preparations. The crew went on Amber Alert for a lift-off as soon as the weather allowed. In Sugar Loaf, Maine, and in the London control center, support teams, friends, and relatives would now have to sit and wait.

Takeoff

The decision when to launch the *Virgin Atlantic Flyer* was to be made on the advice of just one man — the weather expert Bob Rice.

Getting exactly the right weather conditions was the most important part of the flight. A balloon cannot steer itself; it has to go where the wind blows it. So, the wind had to blow in exactly the right direction and at exactly the right speed to carry the balloon across the Atlantic.

Just as important, the conditions on the ground, at the launch site, had to be right also. Nobody had ever blown up a balloon of this size before. Everybody knew how fragile the balloon material was. One small gust of wind at the wrong time and the whole project would be over.

Working out of his office at Weather Services Corporation, Bedford, Massachusetts, Bob Rice has controlled most of the successful long distance balloon flights of the last 20 years. He knew that launching too early could prove disastrous. And so, he made everybody wait.

He made everybody wait for almost ten days before he finally saw what he hoped were the right weather conditions. It was raining in Sugar Loaf, but Bob Rice predicted calm, clear conditions for the morning of Thursday, July 2. Takeoff would be just before dawn, and the wind across the Atlantic looked good.

As the final countdown began, the balloon's massive envelope was fully unrolled for the first time. The **inflation** of the envelope was going to take several hours and began in the darkness, just after midnight.

First the neck of the balloon was held open and cold air blown in to stretch the fabric out. Then, with the full balloon laid out on the grass, the first burner was lit. The delicate process of warming the air inside the balloon had begun.

Around the launch site the 40-person ground crew held their breath as the envelope began to take shape. Under the direction of Tom Barrow, they worked slowly and carefully, checking every move. Nobody had ever inflated a balloon of this size before. Nobody knew what to expect.

In the hotel the two pilots were awakened to be told that all was going well. They had breakfast and a police escort took the small team down to the launch site. There, in the cold light of pre-dawn, the *Virgin Atlantic Flyer* stood, upright and fully inflated. The burners were on. She was ready for takeoff.

There was just time for a few last farewells, and then the two pilots climbed on board. Final checks were made; the flight systems tested; the weather reports read again. On the ground, Tom Barrow gave the

Richard Branson and Per Lindstrand on their way to launch

Waiting at Sugar Loaf for the good weather

signal and, in the capsule, Per Lindstrand turned the burners on to full power.

At 4:10 in the morning, with dawn breaking over the Maine countryside, the *Virgin Atlantic Flyer* began to lift. The ground crew held the final stabilizing ropes for a few seconds more and then let go. The balloon was airborne.

Then, for a moment, there was panic. As the balloon lifted off, a gas tank broke free and crashed to the ground. People scattered, fearing an explosion but it never came. Looking up, they saw that the balloon seemed undamaged, but it was carrying extra weight. A sandbag, used to help keep the balloon on the ground, had failed to fall off. It didn't seem too serious.

On the ground, the relief was immense. The weather was perfect. The balloon was climbing fast. The Atlantic challenge was under way.

They're away

In Flight

Full power as dawn comes up

Losing a gas cylinder at takeoff looked dramatic from the ground but did not worry the pilots. For reasons of safety, the *Flyer* had been designed to carry more gas than it needed. The wind speeds were good and the course across the ocean was set.

The sandbag, which was still attached, was considerably more trouble. Not only did it cause unnecessary weight during the climb; it also caused an unnecessary tilt. Per Lindstrand decided that he would have to climb out of the capsule to cut it off.

As soon as it was light enough and he could see, he stepped out of the door and around the capsule, hanging onto the railing with one hand. Then he cut the sandbag free with the other hand.

Without the weight of the sandbag, the balloon began to climb steadily and quickly to the planned cruising height. Two small aircraft, which were filming the climb, were left behind as the *Virgin Atlantic Flyer* reached 27,000 feet above Nova Scotia and began its historic voyage. Everything was going smoothly.

Past Halifax and approaching St. John's, Newfoundland, just around New Brunswick, there was the first hiccup in the flight. Suddenly there was a massive bang, and the balloon jerked upwards. The pilots checked the instruments. They thought that the balloon must have hit something. Then the radio crackled into life.

A supersonic *Concorde* aircraft flying from New York to London had passed over the top of them. The shock wave from the *Concorde* had almost blown the *Flyer* out of the sky, even though the airplane was some 30,000 feet higher.

Worried that more airplanes would pass by and have the same effect, Per Lindstrand radioed the *Concorde* pilots and arranged that future planes would give at least one minute's warning before flying overhead.

Coming in over the coast

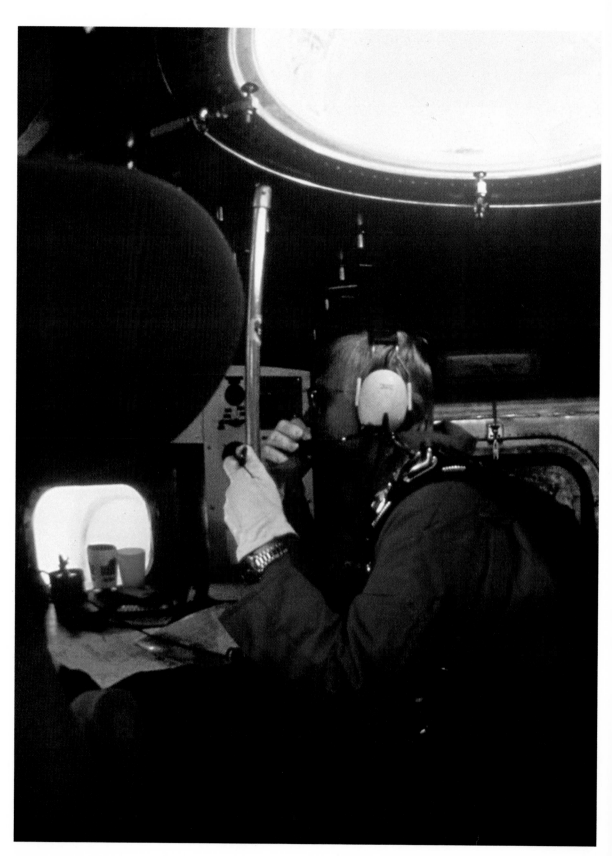

Dawn over the coast of the USA
(Picture: Boston Globe)

Ten hours and three minutes into the flight, the pilots plotted their position as 914 miles from the launch site. Already they had broken the hot air balloon long distance record and were clear of the coast off St. John's, Newfoundland. Now they were properly over the Atlantic.

About 200 miles out into the ocean they hit the first bad storm that weatherman, Bob Rice, had predicted. There was no way to climb above it; the key to survival was to fly through it.

Nobody had ever flown a balloon through a storm like this before, but the pilots had to trust their skills. It was snowing. It was dark. The balloon kept shaking. There was the danger of electrical storms. And the burners were on full power because there was no sunlight in the clouds.

They stuck to a height of 27,000 feet and for three hours it was dreadful. Then they broke through into brilliant sunshine.

At that moment, Lindstrand knew that they were going to make it. If the balloon could survive such a violent storm and still be flying, it would survive anything. There was another magical moment, just before dawn, when they passed the mid-point of the Atlantic.

Whatever that balloon had done then, whatever problems had occurred, however much fuel they had started to use, they were going to scrape home, one way or another. Nobody was going to rob them of that flight.

Per Lindstrand working inside the capsule

Crash Landing

At 2:33 on the afternoon of Friday, July 3, *Virgin Atlantic Flyer* flew over the coast of Ireland on the eastern edge of the Atlantic. It had taken only 29 hours and 23 minutes to achieve the first crossing by hot air balloon.

For the first time, Per Lindstrand had to think about the landing. The biggest problem was what to do about the gasoline that had not been used during the flight. Only two gas tanks had been emptied during the whole crossing — there were still three full gas tanks attached to the capsule.

With a layer of cloud below them, and no exact weather report for Northern Ireland, the two men decided to come down to drop the gas tanks over open country. With the hot air burners switched off,

Trying to land in the sea

the giant balloon began to descend toward the earth.

Everything went according to plan, except that the balloon was coming down faster than either of the crew men realized. Instead of drifting to a soft landing, the capsule crashed hard into a field near **Limavady**, narrowly missing the top of a farm house.

The force of the landing broke the gas tanks away from the capsule. Without the weight of two and a half tons of gas, the balloon took off again like a rocket. Helpless in the capsule, Lindstrand and Branson could only hang on until the *Virgin Atlantic Flyer* found its own way back to stable flight.

They had touched the ground and so, officially, they had crossed the sea. The distance they had covered was a new world record of 3,075 miles. Now the best thing to do was to get safely down as soon

Rescued by a local fishing boat

as possible. It was decided that they would try to land on a beach but their luck had deserted them.

The *Virgin Atlantic Flyer* missed the beach completely and hit the water about half a mile out to sea. Balloon and crew were helpless as the strong wind started to blow them away from the coast, farther and farther away from safety.

Both men knew that there was a danger of the capsule sinking under the waves as they were swept along. 'Jump; get out now. Jump quickly,' ordered Lindstrand as he threw himself over the side of the capsule and into the water. Branson was not quick enough.

The balloon took off again and was soon back at 15,000 feet. Now Branson was alone. He strapped on his parachute and thought about throwing himself out, but he realized that his chances of living were better if he stayed with the capsule.

Slowly he brought the *Flyer* back under control again and, as he came down through the clouds, he saw a British navy ship, HMS *Argonaut,* circling in the water below. He crashed the capsule back into the sea and jumped.

But what of Per Lindstrand? Nobody, apart from Branson, had realized that he was in the water. Immediately, a massive search was launched for the brave pilot, now swimming in cold waters of the Atlantic Ocean. Over one hour after he had jumped, Per was seen by a rescue helicopter and then picked up by a small boat. Both Per and Richard were safe and alive.

The first crossing of the Atlantic Ocean by hot air balloon had come to a dramatic end. The *Virgin Atlantic Flyer* was damaged beyond repair by the crash landing, but it had beaten all the world records and set a new challenge for the next generation of balloon pilots. The Atlantic Ocean had been crossed.

Glossary

Altitude: The height of an object above sea level.

Balloon: The earliest flying machine invented by man, consisting of an envelope and a basket.

Basket: The part of a balloon in which the passengers travel.

Burners: Flames used to heat the air in a balloon.

Capsule: An enclosed container in which the pilot and crew ride.

Concorde: A jet aircraft which flies the Atlantic faster than the speed of sound.

Envelope: The part of the balloon filled with air or gas that lifts the basket and pilots.

Free-fall: A method of parachuting that allows you to escape from an airplane at great height.

Generator: An engine for making electricity.

Helium: A gas lighter than air that is used to inflate some balloons.

Hydrogen: A gas lighter than air that is used to inflate some balloons.

Limavady, Northern Ireland: The small town near which *Virgin Atlantic Flyer* landed.

Parachute: A device that allows a pilot to land safely after jumping out of an airplane.

Propane: A gas that is used in the burners of hot air balloons.

Solar power: Power made by using the heat of the sun.

Sugar Loaf, Maine: The ski resort in the U.S. that was the launch site for *Virgin Atlantic Flyer.*

BALLOON VOYAGE

Index